Lolly's Diary

In loving memory

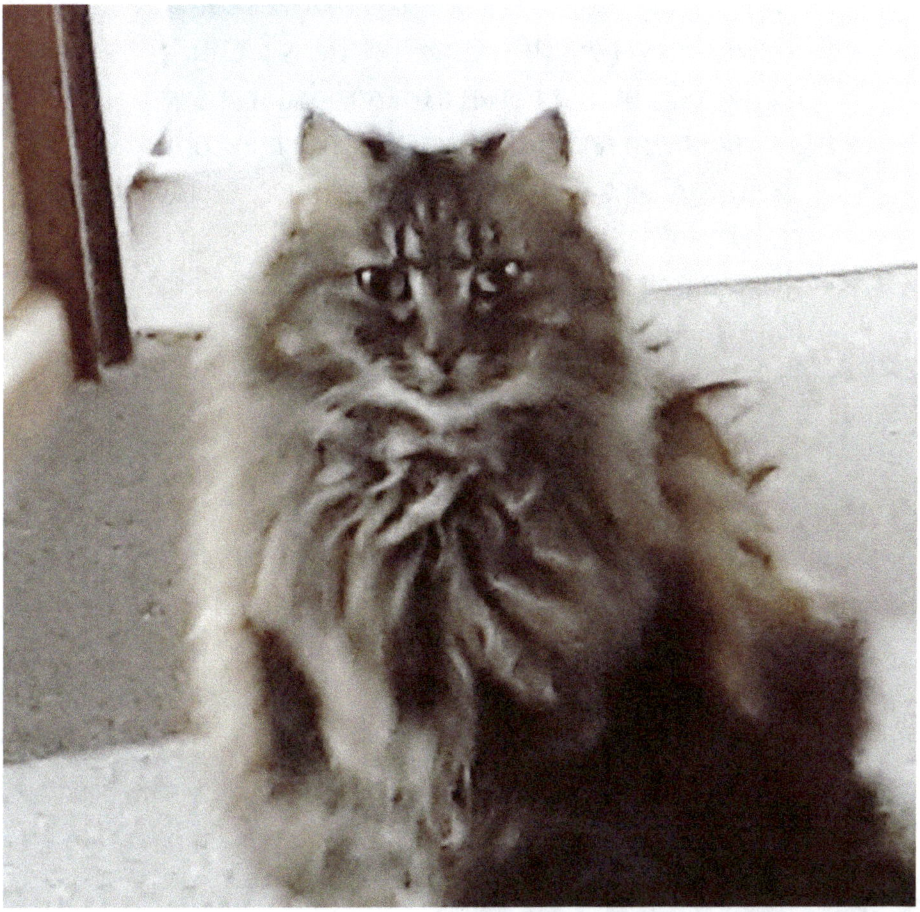

Lolly Wiggins

Written by:
Madelyn Lahey

Illustrated by:
Laura Woodriff

Hi-Hello. My name is Lolly Wiggins and, this is my first time writing in a diary. I heard diaries are supposed to be secret, but I don't want this to be secret. I want people to know about me, and the things that I feel like writing; about things that happen in my life.

While my big sister (Madelyn) says that her cat Delilah has a hard life, I think that life is pretty darn good! I have a human mum and dad that love me very much and spoil me plenty. They bring other humans around and they socialise with me; I couldn't be happier. They feed me lots of yummy food and dad likes to play chasings with me, and sometimes I like to play with him. I like to bite him and he asks, "Why you biting me for?" I bite him because it's fun.

My mum's the best mum ever. She pampers me and feeds me and makes me feel like the most loved cat in the world. And then there's my big sister who loves me and feeds me chippies.
I love chippies! But more on that later because I'm running out of page.
Heehee!

People tell me I'm small and tiny and that I should act my age, but they clearly don't see me for who I am: A QUEEN! When I look at myself in the mirror, I don't see a cat that's smaller than normal; I see a tall, powerful presence who rules over the kingdom of the Wiggins with a respectful fist. I love my subjects just as much as they love me. They like to ensure my safety and wellbeing and I'm fed nothing but the best of foods. I may be small on the outside, but inside I'm the biggest of cats you could meet.

Dad is the best! I love to play with him because he makes me feel so special and reminds me every day of how special I am and how I impact his life in positive ways.. I love it when he comes home and I'm outside because he gives me that whistle which tells me he's come home and is ready for a cuddle. I love cuddling with him, especially when he puts me on his shoulder and caresses me like I'm the only thing in the world that matters to him.

I swear I don't belong in here.
Though it is cosy

Okay, mum's being mean. She took away the nice outdoor seating that I loved to lie under, and I'm reduced to sleeping in a bucket, yes, a bucket, though not just any old bucket, a nice bucket, a bucket that I feel safe in. I sure hope Mum doesn't take this away from me.

Dear Diary. No.6

Mum took the bucket from me...

I just remembered the first time I met Delilah.
She was a meanie. Big Sis brought me into the bathroom where she was and Delilah instantly decided I was enemy Number One and picked a fight with me. I mean, the sheer audacity of her! I wasn't going to do anything unless I provoked. Needless to say, she provoked me, it was Big Sis that had to break us up. I retreated outside while Delilah stayed inside. I don't like Delilah. She's mean.

Look at me... look at my fur, it-it's ruined!
I thought Big Sis and I were besties. We did everything together! We were chums until today when she picked me up, took me, and put me in the shower. That's when it comes to me; when I realise what she's going to do to me. NOOOOO!!! Shower time is the worst! Especially when it's dad who tells Big Sis to go through with it Why Dad, why? How could you betray me like this?

I love my mum, because even though she's busy, she always puts my needs first (as she should) and feeds me, giving me Temptation treats — which I love— and puts wet food into my bowl, though if I'm being honest, I like the dry food better.

Whatever, I can talk about food another time. This time I'm going to talk about Mum and how I love her. Like Dad, I love cuddling up on her shoulder and I love sleeping above her head at night and by her feet when she's asleep. Like Dad and Big Sis, Mum tells me I'm special and reminds me whenever she comes home that I'm the perfect cat.

Sorry, I can't write right now, getting pampered by Dad.

Okay, sorry if that last one was short—
I was just in the process of being pampered by one of the best people I know: Dad. He truly is a remarkable and wonderful human soul. Like I said in my previous diary entry, he makes me feel so special. I'd be lying if I said I don't love it when he whistles and calls out my name like I'm a dog. Whoever said behaving like a dog is a bad thing? I certainly didn't. If I'm being honest, acting like a dog and having more energy and life in you is more fun than sleeping all day. It means that I'm always awake for the times dad comes home ready for a cuddle.

Dear Diary. No.12

Just in case I haven't written about this before. I may be small, but I have a BIG personality, and I don't let anything I don't like stand in my way, not even this annoying grey cat that often likes to intrude on my kingdom. I quickly make him/her run away as soon as I see him/her

I love it when it's Christmas, because that means a lot of yummy food, lots of people to play with and, of course, spending time with my family.

Ugggghhhhh... soooo full...
Why did I eat so much of that chicken?

Mmmm.. Yumyumyum...
this pool water is just the right temperature.

Dear Diary. No.16
Zzzzzzzzzzzzzz chips... zzzzzzzzzzzz

Dear Diary No. 17

I like to sleep on newspapers. They may seem uncomfortable, but we cats like to sleep on anything we can fit on. And because of my little size, I can fit on anything.

I'm going to sleep now,
so thank you for reading about me.

Copyright@Madelyn Lahey (2025)

The right of Chantelle Jacqueline to be identified as author of this work has been asserted by her in accordance with section 77 and78 of the Copyright, Designs and Patents Act 1988.

All rights reserved. No part of this publication may be reproduced, stored in a retrieval system, or transmitted in any form or by any means, electronic, mechanical, photocopying, recording, or otherwise, without the prior permission of the publishers.

Any person who commits any unauthorised act in relation to this publication may be liable to criminal prosecution and civil claims for damages.

ISBN 9780648408567 (Paperback)

First Published (2025)

www.ingramcontent.com/pod-product-compliance
Lightning Source LLC
Chambersburg PA
CBHW051216290426
44109CB00021B/2475